INDIAN COOKING

Naomi Good

CHANCELLOR
PRESS

CONTENTS

First published in Great Britain in 1984
This edition published in 1993 by Chancellor Press
an imprint of Reed Consumer Books Limited
Michelin House, 81 Fulham Road, London SW3 6RB
and Auckland, Melbourne, Singapore and Toronto
Reprinted 1993 (twice)
Copyright © 1984 Reed International Books Limited
ISBN 1 85152 320 0
A CIP catalogue record for this book is available from the
British Library
Printed in Hong Kong

NOTES

Standard spoon measurements are
used in all recipes.
1 tablespoon = one 15 ml spoon
1 teaspoon = one 5 ml spoon
All spoon measures are level.

Use freshly ground black pepper
where pepper is specified.
Use whole black peppercorns
where peppercorns are specified.

Ovens should be preheated to the
specified temperature.

For all recipes, quantities are given
in both metric and imperial
measures. Follow either set but not
a mixture of both, because they are
not interchangeable.

Ingredients marked with an
asterisk are explained on
pages 8 to 11.

INTRODUCTION

The splendid thing about Indian cooking is that most of the recipes can be prepared in advance and the dishes then heated just before serving without coming to any harm.

A simple methodical approach to preparing Indian food also makes entertaining easier. Assemble all the ingredients needed for the recipe before you begin to cook. Measure out all the spices and seasonings and put them on a plate in separate piles. Chop, slice, grate or process fresh ingredients and have them ready on your board. The recipe will then be very simple to follow with everything to hand.

A traditional Indian family meal usually consists of one meat, poultry or fish dish, one vegetable dish, and one lentil dish, served with rice or bread and accompanied by yogurt, and chutneys or pickles. Desserts are not usually served for everyday meals.

When entertaining, an extra meat or fish dish and an additional vegetable dish will be served and the meal ended with a dessert or a selection of sweetmeats.

It is important that the chosen dishes contrast with each other in colour, texture and flavour. This balance makes the meal attractive to both the eye and the palate and gives the meal its typical Indian zest.

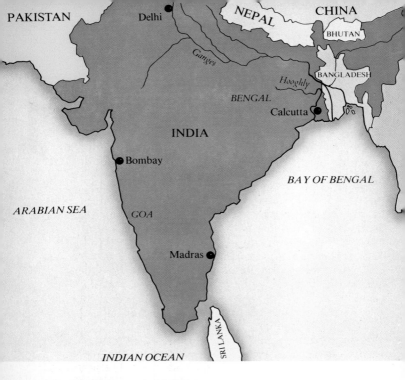

REGIONAL COOKING

India is a large country with many regional variations in climate, custom, religion and food. The country has been invaded and colonized many times, and each time changes have taken place in the eating habits of the local population.

When the Moguls descended on northern India in the sixteenth century they brought with them their rich meat-based cuisine. From central Asia, too, came the *tandoor*, the clay oven, which gives its name to those delectable dishes now served in every Indian restaurant.

The north is a wheat-growing, bread-eating area. The preferred cooking fat is ghee*, although substitutes are used. Generally speaking the food is mild; it gets progressively hotter and spicier the farther south you go.

The population of India is predominantly Hindu and vegetarian. When Hindus eat meat it is usually lamb – never beef, for the cow is sacred. There are, of course, many meat-eating minorities: the Goans from the ex-Portuguese colony on the west coast for whom pork is a speciality; the Muslims who eat beef and lamb but never pork; the Parsees who are omnivorous.

The more southern states grow rice as their staple food, use oil in preference to ghee and tend to be vegetarian. In Bengal on the east coast the food is again different, as they

6

have plenty of fish – especially plump king-size prawns and lobsters – in the tidal waters of the Hooghly river. Mustard seeds and mustard oil are popular here too. But best of all are their sweets – little white and brown spheres floating in syrup and fudge-like pink, white and green squares.

All Indians love sweets but leave the making of them to the professionals. Those sweets that are simple enough to be made at home require patience rather than skill and the full attention of the cook or the results will be disappointing.

EQUIPMENT

In India the traditional method of grinding spices to a paste or powder is in a large mortar or on a flat stone using a heavy rolling-pin shaped stone. Here an electric blender with a strong motor or a food processor will make quick work of puréeing spices.

To grind small quantities of dry spices a coffee grinder is ideal – but you will not be able to use it for grinding coffee again. If you do not have a blender, a mezzaluna (a curved blade with two handles), a garlic press and a grater will give very satisfactory results.

In India saucepans do not have handles. They used to be made of heavy copper with tinned interiors and curved bottoms, but now they are often made from aluminium and are flat bottomed.

For frying, a large heavy wok-like pan is used and for making bread a slightly curved, iron plate-like griddle. Any heavy frying pan can be used instead.

In a traditional Indian household plates are not used. Instead they serve food on *thalis*, round trays made from metal, usually brass although stainless steel is becoming more commonly used especially in urban areas, and silver (by those who can afford it) for special occasions. Small bowls called *katoris* are placed on the tray and filled with the various dishes. Chutneys and accompaniments are arranged on the *thali* itself as are breads such as puris or chapatis. Rice is also served directly on to the tray. In the south banana leaves are sometimes used and make delightful disposable *thalis*.

At the end of a meal, especially if it has been a heavy one, *paan* is served as a *digestif* and an astringent mouth freshener. *Paan* is made from the leaf of the betel palm, spread with lime (calcium) paste and filled with chopped betel nut and a variety of spices such as cloves, cardamom seeds and aniseed. The leaf is then neatly folded into a triangle small enough to be popped whole into the mouth. It turns the mouth red when chewed and is addictive especially when the ingredients include tobacco.

SPECIALIST INGREDIENTS

The following are available from Asian food stores and
other specialist shops, some supermarkets, delicatessens and
greengrocers:

Cardamom (elaichi) An aromatic seed pod which comes in three
varieties: white, green (more perfumed than the white) and large
black (not always available). The whole pod is used to flavour rice
and meat dishes and then discarded, or the pod is opened and the
seeds removed and crushed for sprinkling on sweets or vegetables.

Cayenne pepper or chilli powder Powdered dried red chillies.
The strength varies from batch to batch. Use with caution.

Chillies, hot fresh green (hari mirch) Use with care. For a less
pungent result slit the chillies and discard the seeds. Do not touch
your face or rub your eyes while handling chillies, and wash your
hands immediately afterwards.

Chillies, dried red (sabat lal mirch) These add a good flavour
when tossed in whole with other frying spices. The smaller ones
are very pungent so add them cautiously. They can also be
crumbled between finger tips, if preferred. Handle with the same
care as green chillies (above).

Cinnamon (dalchini) Available in stick and ground form. The
stick should be discarded before the dish is served.

Coconut (narial) Used in many sweet and savoury dishes. When
buying a coconut choose one that is heavy for its size. To open it,
pierce the 'eyes' with a skewer and pour away the liquid. Put the
coconut in a preheated moderately hot oven, 190°C (375°F), Gas
Mark 5, for 15 minutes, then place on a sturdy table or on the floor
and give it a sharp tap with a mallet or hammer; it will break in
two. Using a sharp knife, prise away the flesh from the shell, then
peel off the brown skin and cut the coconut into pieces.

   If the coconut is already open – Indian shopkeepers will do it for
you – put it in the oven for 15 to 20 minutes or until you hear the
shell cracking. The flesh will then be easy to remove.

Grate the coconut in a food processor or by hand and use as required.

Coconut milk is an infusion used to flavour and thicken many dishes, particularly in Southern India. To make coconut milk, place the grated coconut in a bowl, pour over about 600 ml (1 pint) boiling water, just to cover and leave for 1 hour. Strain through muslin, squeezing hard to extract as much 'milk' as possible. This is called 'thick' coconut milk. To make 'thin' coconut milk pour another 600 ml (1 pint) of boiling water over the coconut flesh from which the thick milk has already been extracted, and repeat the process.

Bought creamed coconut is a very useful substitute.

Coriander, fresh green (hara dhanya) A delicate, fragrant herb. Used chopped to sprinkle over dishes as a garnish or stirred in at the end of the cooking time or puréed to make sauces and chutneys. Parsley may be substituted, but it doesn't have the same flavour.

Coriander seeds (dhanya) Come whole or ground. Used a lot in ground form. Very fragrant.

Cumin seeds (zeera) There are many varieties of this strong flavoured, caraway-like seed. The black variety is best. Comes ground or whole.

Curry leaves (kari patta) Aromatic leaves of the sweet Nim tree, available dried. They release a very appetizing smell when cooked.

Fennel seeds (sonf) These aniseed-flavoured seeds are often chewed as a digestive. They add a fine flavour and aroma to many dishes.

Garam Masala A ground spice mixture used in many recipes. You can buy it or prepare your own: the flavour is obviously better when it is freshly ground. To make garam masala, place 2 tablespoons black peppercorns, 1 tablespoon black cumin seeds, 1 small cinnamon stick, 1 teaspoon whole cloves, ¼ nutmeg, 2 teaspoons cardamom seeds and 2 tablespoons coriander seeds in a coffee grinder and grind to a powder. Store in a screw-topped jar.

Ghee (clarified butter) A good cooking fat. It is better than butter because it can be heated to a higher temperature without burning. Ghee can be bought in tins or made at home. To make ghee, place 250 g (8 oz) unsalted butter in a small pan over low heat. Bring to just below simmering point and cook for 20 to 30 minutes or until it has stopped sputtering and is beginning to change colour. Strain through several thicknesses of muslin. Keep in a screw-topped jar in a cool place – refrigeration is not necessary.

250 g (8 oz) butter makes 175–200 ml (6–7 fl oz) ghee. Larger quantities take a little longer to make.

Ginger, fresh (adrak) A khaki-coloured, knobbly rhizome. Should be smooth and fresh looking. Keep in a plastic bag in the refrigerator. Always peel before using. It can be grated, finely chopped or puréed in an electric blender or food processor.

Ginger, dried (sonth) Sold whole or powdered. Does not give as good a flavour as fresh ginger.

Gram flour (bessan) Ground chick peas or split peas. Excellent for making batter and used in place of flour.

Mustard seeds (sarson) Small, round reddish–black seeds. When fried for a few seconds they sputter with the heat and give out a delicious smell.

Oil Use any vegetable oil for cooking Indian food. Ground nut oil is commonly used in India.

Panir (Indian cheese) A curd cheese used in cooking. To make panir, bring 1.2 litres (2 pints) milk to the boil, remove from heat and stir in a bare ¼ teaspoon tartaric acid dissolved in 120 ml (4 fl oz) hot water. Stir gently until the milk curdles, then leave for 30 minutes. Line a sieve with muslin and strain the curdled milk, squeezing out all the liquid. Form the remaining curds into a rough rectangle about 1–1.5 cm (½–¾ inch) deep in the same cloth and wrap it tightly round. Place this packet between two flat surfaces and place a 2.5 kg (5 lb) weight on top. Leave for 2 to 3 hours. 1.2 litres (2 pints) milk makes 125 g (4 oz) panir.

Pulses (dhals) These form an important part of the Indian diet. There are nearly 60 varieties in India but the most commonly used are mung, both olive green and yellow; *masoor* or Egyptian lentils – the common salmon pink lentils available in every supermarket; *channa* – split peas; *kabli channa* or Bengal gram – whole peas; *tur* – the vari-coloured pigeon-pea; *lobia* – black-eyed peas; and *rajma* – red kidney beans.

Saffron (kesar) Available in threads and in powdered form. The threads are soaked in hot water or milk before using. Saffron gives food a lovely yellow colour and a fine aroma and taste. Expensive but worth it.

Sesame seeds (til) These have a fine nutty flavour. They are used to flavour some vegetable dishes and to sprinkle on *naan*.

Tamarind (imli) Pods from the tamarind tree, used as a souring agent. Sold as pods or pulp – pulp is easier to use. Both must be soaked in hot water, then squeezed and strained before use. Vinegar or lemon juice may be used instead.

Turmeric (haldi) A rhizome commonly used in its powdered form for its earthy taste and yellow colour. It stains clothing and work surfaces so be careful not to spill it.

Yogurt (dhai) Yogurt is eaten daily all over India, either plain or with vegetables or fruit mixed in. It is also used in cooking, particularly in the north. Yogurt is quite easy to make at home, using a special machine or electric oven.

To make yogurt, bring 600 ml (1 pint) milk to the boil. As the milk begins to rise in the pan, take it off the heat and dip the pan in cold water to cool. Put 2 teaspoons bought natural yogurt in a heatproof bowl and stir well. Pour over the warm milk and mix well. Place in a preheated very cool oven – as low as your oven will go – and leave for 30 minutes. Turn off the heat and leave the bowl in the oven for 5 hours or until the yogurt is set, switching the heat on and off as necessary during this time to maintain the temperature.

SAVOURIES

Ekuri

50 g (2 oz) butter
1 onion, finely
    chopped
2 green chillies*,
    finely chopped
8 eggs, lightly beaten
    with 2 tablespoons
    water
1 tablespoon finely
    chopped coriander*
salt

Heat the butter in a pan, add the onion and fry until deep golden. Add the chillies and fry for 30 seconds, then add the eggs, coriander and salt to taste, and cook, stirring, until the eggs are scrambled and set. Serve hot.
Serves 4

Shish Kebab

500 g (1 lb) minced
    lamb
2 tablespoons finely
    chopped celery
    leaves
2 tablespoons
    chopped parsley
2 onions, finely
    chopped
1 teaspoon turmeric*
salt and pepper
TO GARNISH:
chopped parsley
finely chopped onion

Mix all the ingredients together very thoroughly, seasoning with salt and pepper to taste. Roll the mixture into thin sausage shapes and cook under a preheated moderate grill for about 10 minutes, turning several times. Serve garnished with parsley and chopped onion.

Serves 4

Pakora

125 g (4 oz) gram
  flour*
1 teaspoon salt
½ teaspoon chilli
  powder*
about 150 ml (¼
  pint) water
2 green chillies*,
  finely chopped
1 tablespoon finely
  chopped coriander*
1 teaspoon melted
  butter or ghee*
2 onions, cut into
  rings
oil for deep-frying
8 small fresh spinach
  leaves
2-3 potatoes, par-
  boiled and sliced

Sift the flour, salt and chilli powder into a bowl. Stir in sufficient water to make a thick batter and beat well until smooth. Leave to stand for 30 minutes.

Stir the chillies and coriander into the batter, then add the melted butter or ghee. Drop in the onion rings to coat thickly with batter.

Heat the oil in a deep pan, drop in the onion rings and deep-fry until crisp and golden. Remove from the pan with a slotted spoon, drain on kitchen paper and keep warm.

Dip the spinach leaves into the batter and deep-fry in the same way, adding more oil to the pan if necessary.

Finally, repeat the process with the potato slices.

Serve hot.

Serves 4

Chicken Tikka

150 g (5.2 oz)
  natural yogurt
1 tablespoon grated
  ginger*
2 cloves garlic,
  crushed
1 teaspoon chilli
  powder*
1 tablespoon ground
  coriander seeds*
½ teaspoon salt
juice of 1 lemon
2 tablespoons oil
750 (1½ lb) chicken
  breasts, skinned
  and boned

TO GARNISH:
1 onion, sliced
2 tomatoes, quartered
4 lemon twists

Mix together in a bowl all the ingredients except the chicken. Cut the chicken into cubes and drop into the marinade. Cover and leave in the refrigerator overnight.

Thread the chicken on to 4 skewers and cook under a preheated hot grill for 5 to 6 minutes, turning frequently.

Remove the chicken from the skewers and arrange on individual serving plates. Garnish with onion, tomato and lemon to serve.

Serves 4

Meat Samosa

PASTRY:

*125 g (4 oz) plain
    flour*
¼ teaspoon salt
25 g (1 oz) ghee or
    butter*
2-3 tablespoons water

FILLING:

1 tablespoon oil
1 small onion, minced
1 clove garlic, crushed
1 green chilli ,
    minced*
*½ teaspoon chilli
    powder**
*250 g (8 oz) minced
    beef*
*125 g (4 oz) tomato,
    skinned and
    chopped*
*1 tablespoon chopped
    coriander**
salt

oil for deep-frying

Sift the flour and salt into a mixing bowl. Rub in the ghee or butter until the mixture resembles breadcrumbs. Add the water and knead thoroughly to a very smooth dough. Cover and chill while preparing the filling.

Heat the oil in a pan, add the onion and garlic and fry until golden. Add the chilli and chilli powder and fry for 3 minutes. Stir in the meat and cook until well browned. Add the tomato, coriander, and salt to taste and simmer gently for 20 minutes, until the meat is tender and the mixture is dry; skim off any fat. Stir well and cool slightly.

Divide the pastry into 8 pieces. Dust with flour and roll each piece into a thin round, then cut each round in half. Fold each half into a cone and brush the seam with water to seal.

Fill the cone with a spoonful of filling (do not overfill), dampen the top edge and seal firmly. Deep-fry until crisp and golden. Serve hot or warm.

Serves 4

Vegetable Samosa

PASTRY:

125 g (4 oz) plain
  flour
¼ teaspoon salt
25 g (1 oz) ghee* or
  butter
2-3 tablespoons water

FILLING:

1 tablespoon oil
1 teaspoon mustard
  seeds*
1 small onion, minced
2 green chillies*,
  minced
¼ teaspoon turmeric*
1 teaspoon finely
  chopped ginger*
salt
125 g (4 oz) frozen
  peas
125 g (4 oz) cooked
  potatoes, diced
½ tablespoon
  chopped coriander*
1 tablespoon lemon
  juice
oil for deep-frying

Make the pastry as for Meat Samosa
(opposite). Chill while preparing the
filling.

Heat the oil in a pan and add the
mustard seeds. Leave for a few
seconds until they start to pop, then
add the onion and fry until golden.
Add the chillies, turmeric, ginger,
and salt to taste and fry for 3 minutes;
if it starts sticking to the pan add
½ tablespoon water and stir well.
Add the peas, stir well and cook for
2 minutes. Add the potatoes and
coriander, stir well and cook for
1 minute. Stir in the lemon juice.
Cool slightly.

Shape and cook as for Meat
Samosa. Serve hot or warm.
Serves 4

MEAT DISHES

Meat Puffs

3 tablespoons self-
  raising flour
3 eggs, beaten
5-6 tablespoons water
250 g (8 oz) minced
  beef
1 bunch of spring
  onions, finely
  sliced
1 green chilli*, finely
  chopped
1 teaspoon turmeric*
salt
oil for frying

Sift the flour into a bowl, add the eggs and beat well to combine. Gradually add enough water to make a thick creamy batter, beating well.

Stir in the minced beef, onions, chilli, turmeric, and salt to taste; the mixture should be like a stiff porridge. Leave in a warm place for 1 hour.

Heat about 1 cm (½ inch) depth of oil in a frying pan. When really hot, drop in spoonfuls of the meat mixture and fry on each side for 2 minutes. Drain well and keep warm while cooking the remainder, adding more oil as required. Serve hot.
Serves 4

Brinjal Cutlets

2 large aubergines
salt
3 tablespoons oil
1 onion, finely
    chopped
1 clove garlic, finely
    chopped
2 green chillies*,
    seeded and finely
    chopped
1 teaspoon turmeric*
500 g (1 lb) minced
    beef
1 egg, lightly beaten
2-3 tablespoons fresh
    breadcrumbs

Cook the aubergines in boiling salted water for 15 minutes or until almost tender. Drain thoroughly and cool.

Heat the oil in a pan, add the onion and fry until golden. Add the garlic, chillies and turmeric and fry for 2 minutes. Add the mince and cook, stirring, until brown all over. Add salt to taste and cook gently for 20 minutes, until the meat is tender.

Cut the aubergines in half lengthways. Carefully scoop out the pulp, add it to the meat mixture and mix well. Check the seasoning. Fill the aubergine shells with the mixture, brush with egg and cover with breadcrumbs. Cook under a preheated moderate grill for 4 to 5 minutes, until golden.
Serves 4

Kheema with Potatoes and Peas

4 tablespoons oil
2 onions, finely
  chopped
2 teaspoons ground
  coriander seeds*
1/2 teaspoon ground
  cumin seeds*
1/2 teaspoon ground
  turmeric*
2.5 cm (1 inch) piece
  ginger*, finely
  chopped
1 chilli*, finely
  chopped
1 heaped teaspoon
  garam masala*
500 g (1 lb) minced
  beef
250 g (8 oz) small
  potatoes, quartered
salt
500 g (1 lb) shelled
  peas

Heat the oil in a lidded frying pan,
add the onions and cook until soft.
Add the spices and fry for 5 minutes
over low heat; add 1 tablespoon water
if the mixture starts to burn. Stir in
the minced beef and cook over high
heat until very well browned.

Lower the heat and add the
potatoes and salt to taste. Cover and
cook gently for 5 minutes, then add
the peas. Continue cooking until the
potatoes and peas are tender. Serve
hot.
Serves 4

Kofta in Yogurt

500 g (1 lb) minced
  beef
75 g (3 oz) fresh
  breadcrumbs
2 green chillies*,
  finely chopped
1 onion, finely
  chopped
2.5 cm (1 inch) piece
  ginger*, finely
  chopped
2 teaspoons ground
  coriander seeds*
salt
1 egg, lightly beaten
oil for frying
500 g (1 lb) natural
  yogurt
2 tablespoons finely
  chopped coriander*

Mix the minced beef, breadcrumbs,
chillies, onion, ginger, ground
coriander, salt to taste and egg
together and shape the mixture into
walnut-sized balls.

Heat the oil in a large pan, add the
meat balls and fry until well browned
and cooked through. Drain carefully.

Pour the yogurt into a serving
bowl and add the meat balls while
still hot. Sprinkle with the chopped
coriander and serve warm.
Serves 4

Chilli Fry

4 tablespoons oil
1 large onion, finely
    chopped
½ teaspoon ground
    coriander seeds*
½ teaspoon turmeric*
2.5 cm (1 inch) piece
    ginger*, finely
    chopped
1 chilli*, chopped
500 g (1 lb) frying
    steak, cut into
    strips about 2.5 ×
    1 cm (1 × 1½ inch)
1 green or red pepper,
    cored, seeded and
    roughly chopped
2 tomatoes, quartered
juice of 1 lemon
salt

Heat the oil in a lidded frying pan, add the onion and fry until soft. Add the coriander, turmeric, ginger and chilli and fry over low heat for 5 minutes; if the mixture becomes dry, add 1 tablespoon water.

Add the steak, increase the heat and cook, stirring, until browned all over. Add the chopped pepper, cover and simmer gently for 5 to 10 minutes, until the meat is tender. Add the tomatoes, lemon juice and salt to taste and cook, uncovered, for 2 to 3 minutes.

Serves 4
NOTE: This dish should be rather dry.

Aloo 'Chops'

3 tablespoons oil
1 large onion, finely
   chopped
1 cm (½ inch) piece
   ginger*, finely
   chopped
1 teaspoon ground
   coriander seeds*
250 g (8 oz) minced
   beef
1 tablespoon raisins
salt
1 tablespoon finely
   chopped coriander*
1 kg (2 lb) potatoes,
   boiled and mashed
   with a little milk
   and salt
flour for coating
oil for shallow frying

Heat the oil in a frying pan, add the onion and ginger and fry until golden. Add the ground coriander and minced beef and fry until brown. Add the raisins and salt to taste and simmer for about 20 minutes, until the meat is cooked. Spoon out any fat in the pan. Stir in the chopped coriander and leave to cool.

Divide the mashed potato into 8 portions. With well floured hands, flatten a portion on one palm, put 3 teaspoons of the meat mixture in the centre and fold the potato over it. Form gently into a round patty shape.

Dip the 'chops' lightly in flour and shallow fry a few at a time in hot oil, until crisp and golden, turning carefully to brown the underside.
Serves 4

23

Stuffed Pimento

5 tablespoons oil
1 onion, finely
   chopped
2 teaspoons ground
   coriander seeds*
1 teaspoon ground
   cumin seeds*
1/2 teaspoon chilli
   powder*
350 g (12 oz) minced
   beef
3 tablespoons long-
   grain rice
salt
4 large green or red
   peppers
1 × 397 g (14 oz)
   can tomatoes

Heat 3 tablespoons of the oil in a saucepan, add the onion and fry until golden. Add the spices and cook for 2 minutes. Add the minced beef and fry, stirring, until browned. Add the rice and salt to taste and cook for 2 minutes. Remove from the heat and leave to cool.

Slice the peppers lengthways and discard the seeds and cores. Fill the pepper shells with the meat mixture.

Heat the remaining oil in a pan just large enough to hold the peppers. Place the peppers in the pan. Pour a little of the tomato juice into each pepper and the remaining juice and tomatoes into the pan, seasoning with salt to taste. Bring to simmering point, cover and cook for about 25 minutes, until the rice is tender.
Serves 4

Beef Curry with Potatoes

4 tablespoons oil
2 onions, finely
    chopped
2 cloves garlic,
    chopped
1 teaspoon chilli
    powder*
1 tablespoon ground
    cumin seeds*
1½ tablespoons
    ground coriander
    seeds*
2.5 cm (1 inch) piece
    ginger*, finely
    chopped
750 g (1½ lb)
    stewing steak, cubed
2 tablespoons tomato
    purée
salt
350 g (12 oz) new
    potatoes
4 green chillies*

Heat the oil in a large pan, add the
onions and fry until lightly coloured.
Add the garlic, chilli powder, cumin,
coriander and ginger and cook gently
for 5 minutes, stirring occasionally;
if the mixture becomes dry, add
2 tablespoons water.

Add the beef and cook, stirring,
until browned all over. Add the
tomato purée, salt to taste and just
enough water to cover the meat; stir
very well. Bring to the boil, cover
and simmer for about 1 hour or until
the meat is almost tender. Add the
potatoes and whole chillies and
simmer until the potatoes are cooked.
Serves 4

Kofta Curry

SAUCE:
3 tablespoons oil
2.5 cm (1 inch) piece
    cinnamon stick*
10 cloves
1 onion, chopped
2 cloves garlic, finely
    chopped
5 cm (2 inch) piece
    ginger*, chopped
1 tablespoon ground
    cumin seeds*
2 tablespoons ground
    coriander seeds*
1 teaspoon chilli
    powder*
salt
1 × 397 g (14 oz)
    can tomatoes

KOFTA:
750 g (1½ lb)
    minced beef
2 green chillies*,
    finely chopped
3 tablespoons finely
    chopped coriander*
1 teaspoon garam
    masala*
1 egg, lightly beaten

Heat the oil in a large lidded frying pan. Add the cinnamon and cloves and fry for 30 seconds, then add the onion and fry until golden, stirring occasionally. Add the garlic, ginger, cumin, coriander, chilli powder and salt to taste. Stir well and fry over low heat for 2 minutes, adding 1–2 tablespoons water if the mixture begins to stick. Add the tomatoes with their juice and stir well. Cover and leave to simmer while preparing the Kofta. Mix the Kofta ingredients together, adding salt to taste. With dampened hands, shape the mixture into about 40 walnut-sized balls. Slip them carefully into the sauce in a single layer and simmer very gently for about 30 minutes, turning the meat balls over very carefully every 10 minutes.
Serves 4

Beef Buffad

3 tablespoons oil
2 onions, sliced
2 cloves garlic, finely
 chopped
3 green chillies*,
 chopped
3.5 cm (1½ inch)
 piece ginger*,
 chopped
750 g (1½ lb) braising
 steak, cubed
½ teaspoon chilli
 powder*
1 teaspoon turmeric*
1 teaspoon pepper
1 teaspoon ground
 cumin seeds*
1 tablespoon ground
 coriander seeds*
½ teaspoon ground
 cinnamon*
½ teaspoon ground
 cloves
300 ml (½ pint)
 coconut milk*
 (see note)
salt
150 ml (¼ pint)
 vinegar

Heat the oil in a large saucepan, add the onions and fry until they are just beginning to brown, then add the garlic, chillies and ginger. Fry for 1 minute, then add the beef and remaining spices. Stir well and cook for 5 minutes, stirring occasionally.

Add the coconut milk, which should just cover the meat; if it does not, add a little water. Add salt to taste. Bring to simmering point, cover and cook for about 1½ hours, until the meat is almost tender.

Add the vinegar and continue cooking for about 30 minutes, until the meat is tender and the gravy thick.

Serves 4
NOTE: 75 g (3 oz) creamed coconut*, melted in 250 ml (8 fl oz) warm water, can be used instead of coconut milk.

Nargis Kebab

KEBAB:
250 g (8 oz) ground
    beef or minced
    lamb
2 cloves garlic,
    crushed
2.5 cm (1 inch) piece
    ginger*, grated
½ teaspoon ground
    coriander seeds*
½ teaspoon ground
    cumin seeds*
½-1 teaspoon chilli
    powder*
¼ teaspoon ground
    cloves
1 tablespoon cornflour
salt
1 egg yolk
4 small hard-boiled
    eggs
oil for shallow frying
CURRY SAUCE:
4 tablespoons oil
5 cm (2 inch) piece
    cinnamon stick*
6 cloves
6 cardamom*
1 onion, finely
    chopped
2 cloves garlic,
    crushed
2.5 cm (1 inch) piece
    ginger*, grated
2 teaspoons ground
    coriander seeds*
1 teaspoon ground
    cumin seeds*
½-1 teaspoon chilli
    powder*
4 tablespoons natural
    yogurt
1 × 397 g (14 oz)
    can tomatoes
2 tablespoons
    chopped coriander*

Mix together the meat, garlic, spices, cornflour and salt to taste. Bind with the egg yolk and divide the mixture into 4 equal parts.

With well floured hands, flatten each portion into a round, place a hard-boiled egg in the centre and work the meat round to cover. Roll into a ball.

Heat the oil in a pan and shallow fry the kebabs until they are brown all over. Lift out and set aside while making the sauce.

Heat the oil in a saucepan, add the cinnamon, cloves and cardamom and fry for a few seconds. Add the onion, garlic and ginger and fry until golden brown. Add the coriander, cumin and chilli powder and fry for 1 minute. Add the yogurt, a spoonful at a time, stirring until it is absorbed before adding the next spoonful.

Break up the tomatoes with a fork, add them with their juice and simmer for 1 minute. Add the kebabs to the sauce, season with salt to taste and cook, uncovered, for 25 minutes until the sauce is thick. Stir in the chopped coriander to serve.

Serves 4
NOTE: The kebabs can also be served without the curry sauce, as part of a meal.

Kheema Do Pyaza

500 g (1 lb) onions
4 tablespoons oil
2.5 cm (1 inch) piece
  ginger*, chopped
1 clove garlic, finely
  chopped
2 green chillies*,
  finely chopped
1 teaspoon turmeric*
1 teaspoon ground
  coriander seeds*
1 teaspoon ground
  cumin seeds*
750 g (1½ lb)
  minced lamb
150 g (5.2 oz)
  natural yogurt
1 × 227 g (8 oz) can
  tomatoes
salt

Finely chop 350 g (12 oz) of the onions; thinly slice the remainder.

Heat 2 tablespoons of the oil in a pan, add the chopped onion and fry until golden. Add the ginger, garlic, chillies and spices and fry for 2 minutes. Add the minced lamb and cook, stirring to break up, until well browned.

Stir in the yogurt, spoon by spoon, until it is absorbed, then add the tomatoes with their juice, and salt to taste. Bring to boil, stir well, cover and simmer for 20 minutes or until the meat is cooked.

Meanwhile fry the sliced onions in the remaining oil until brown and crisp.

Transfer the meat mixture to a warmed serving dish and sprinkle with the fried onion.

Serves 4

Lamb Kebab

2 × 150 g (5.2 oz)
  cartons natural
  yogurt
1 tablespoon ground
  coriander seeds*
½ teaspoon chilli
  powder*
1 tablespoon oil
salt
750 g (1½ lb) boned
  leg of lamb, cubed
4 onions
2 red peppers, cored
  and seeded
8 tomatoes
2 tablespoons finely
  chopped coriander*

Put the yogurt, coriander seeds,
chilli, oil, and salt to taste in a large
bowl and stir to combine. Add the
meat, mix well, cover and leave in the
refrigerator overnight.

Cut the onions in quarters and
separate the layers. Cut the peppers
into squares and the tomatoes in half.

Thread the onion, lamb and red
pepper alternately on 8 skewers,
beginning and ending each kebab
with a tomato half. Cook under a
preheated hot grill for about 10
minutes, turning frequently and
basting with any remaining marinade
as necessary. Sprinkle with the
chopped coriander to serve.
Serves 4

Lamb Curry with Coconut

grated flesh of ½
  fresh coconut*
4 dried red chillies*
1 teaspoon cumin seeds*
1 tablespoon
  coriander seeds*
1 tablespoon poppy
  seeds
1 teaspoon peppercorns
2.5 cm (½ inch) piece
  ginger*, chopped
2 cloves garlic
1 teaspoon turmeric*
2 tablespoons lemon
  juice
4 tablespoons oil
2 onions, chopped
4 curry leaves*
750 g (1½ lb) boned
  leg of lamb, cubed
1 × 227g (8 oz) can
  tomatoes
salt
2 tablespoons finely
  chopped coriander*

Heat the coconut, chillies, cumin,
coriander and poppy seeds in a dry
frying pan for about 1 minute. Place
in an electric blender or food
processor with the peppercorns,
ginger, garlic, turmeric and lemon
juice and blend to a paste.

Heat the oil in a pan, add the
onions and fry until soft, then add the
curry leaves and the prepared paste
and fry for 5 minutes. Add the lamb
and cook, stirring, for 5 minutes,
then add the tomatoes with their juice
and salt to taste. Bring to simmering
point, cover and cook for about
1 hour, until tender.

Sprinkle with chopped coriander
to serve.
Serves 4
NOTE: If fresh coconut is not available,
blend the other spices and lemon juice
as above and add 50 g (2 oz) creamed
coconut* to the onions with the
blended spices.

Roghan Ghosht

4 tablespoons oil
2 onions, finely
  chopped
750 g (1½ lb) boned
  leg of lamb, cubed
2 × 150 g (5.2 oz)
  cartons natural
  yogurt
2 cloves garlic
2.5 cm (1 inch) piece
  ginger*
2 green chillies*
1 tablespoon
  coriander seeds*
1 teaspoon cumin
  seeds*
1 teaspoon chopped
  mint leaves
1 teaspoon chopped
  coriander*
6 cardamom*
6 cloves
2.5 cm (1 inch) piece
  cinnamon stick*
salt
125 g (4 oz) flaked
  almonds

Heat 2 tablespoons of the oil in a pan, add one onion and fry until golden. Add the lamb and 175 g (6 oz) of the yogurt, stir well, cover and simmer for 20 minutes.

Place the garlic, ginger, chillies, coriander seeds, cumin, mint, coriander and 2 to 3 tablespoons yogurt in an electric blender or food processor and work to a paste.

Heat the remaining oil in a large saucepan, add the cardamom, cloves and cinnamon and fry for 1 minute, stirring. Add the second onion, prepared paste and fry for 5 minutes, stirring constantly.

Add the lamb and yogurt mixture, and salt to taste, stir well and bring to simmering point. Cover and cook for 30 minutes. Add the almonds and cook for a further 15 minutes, until the meat is tender.

Serves 4

Lamb Curry with Yogurt

4 tablespoons oil
3 onions, finely
  chopped
6 cardamom*
5 cm (2 inch) piece
  cinnamon stick*
1½ tablespoons
  ground coriander
  seeds*
2 teaspoons ground
  cumin seeds*
½ teaspoon turmeric*
½ teaspoon ground
  cloves
1-2 teaspoons chilli
  powder*
½ teaspoon grated
  nutmeg
1 tablespoon paprika
2 × 150 g (5.2 oz)
  cartons natural
  yogurt
750 g (1½ lb) boned
  leg of lamb, cubed
1 large tomato, skinned
  and chopped
salt

Heat the oil in a large saucepan, add the onions, cardamom and cinnamon and fry until onions turn golden. Stir in the coriander, cumin, turmeric, cloves, chilli powder and nutmeg. Fry until dry, then add 2 tablespoons water and cook, stirring, for 5 minutes, adding a little more water if necessary.

Add the paprika and slowly stir in the yogurt. Add the lamb, tomato, and salt to taste and mix well. Bring to simmering point, cover and cook for 1 hour or until the meat is tender.
Serves 4

Lamb Korma

5 tablespoons oil
6 cardamom*
6 cloves
6 peppercorns
2.5 cm (1 inch) piece
   cinnamon stick*
750 g (1½ lb) boned
   leg of lamb, cubed
6 shallots, chopped
2 cloves garlic, finely
   chopped
5 cm (2 inch) piece
   ginger*, chopped
2 tablespoons ground
   coriander seeds*
2 teaspoons ground
   cumin seeds*
1 teaspoon chilli
   powder*
salt
150 g (5.2 oz)
   natural yogurt
1 teaspoon garam
   masala*
2 tablespoons finely
   chopped coriander*
   (optional)

Heat 4 tablespoons of the oil in a pan, add the cardamom, cloves, peppercorns and cinnamon and fry for 1 minute.

Add a few pieces of lamb at a time and fry well to brown all over; transfer to a dish. Remove the whole spices and discard.

Add the remaining oil to the pan and fry the shallots, garlic and ginger for 5 minutes, then add the coriander, cumin, chilli powder, and salt to taste and cook for 5 minutes, stirring to avoid burning. Gradually stir in the yogurt until it is all absorbed.

Return the meat to the pan with any liquid collected in the dish and add sufficient water just to cover the meat. Bring to simmering point, cover and cook for about 1 hour or until the meat is tender.

Sprinkle on the garam masala and cook, stirring, for 1 minute. Top with chopped coriander if using, before serving.

Serves 4

Dry Lamb Curry

750 g (1½ lb) boned
  leg of lamb
3 tablespoons oil
250 g (8 oz) onions,
  finely chopped
6 cloves
6 cardamom
2.5 cm (1 inch) piece
  cinnamon stick*
2 green chillies*,
  finely chopped
2 teaspoons ground
  coriander seeds*
1 teaspoon ground
  cumin seeds*
2 × 150 g (5.2 oz)
  cartons natural
  yogurt
2 tablespoons finely
  chopped coriander*
3 curry leaves*
salt
1 teaspoon garam
  masala*

Cut the lamb into strips.

Heat the oil in a pan, add the onion and fry until soft. Add the cloves, cardamom and cinnamon and fry for 1 minute, then add the chillies and lamb. Fry for a further 10 minutes, turning the lamb to brown on all sides. Add the remaining ingredients, except the garam masala, seasoning with salt to taste. Stir well, bring to simmering point and cook, uncovered, for 40 minutes, until the meat is tender and the liquid evaporated. Stir in the garam masala and serve.

Serves 4

Masala Chops

1 teaspoon ground
  cumin seeds*
2 teaspoons ground
  coriander seeds*
¼ teaspoon chilli
  powder*
1 clove garlic, crushed
salt
lemon juice to mix
4 pork chops

Mix the spices, garlic, and salt to taste
into a paste with lemon juice. Slash
the pork chops on both sides. Rub the
paste into the meat and leave for
30 minutes. Cook under a preheated
moderate grill for 5 or 6 minutes on
each side.
Serves 4

Raan

2.25 kg (5 lb) leg of
  lamb, skin and fat
  removed
50 g (2 oz) fresh
  ginger*, chopped
6 cloves garlic
rind of 1 lemon
juice of 2 lemons
2 teaspoons cumin
  seeds*
6 cardamom*, peeled
1 teaspoon ground
  cloves
1 teaspoon turmeric*
1½ teaspoons chilli
  powder*
1 tablespoon salt
2 × 150 g (5.2 oz)
  cartons natural
  yogurt
150 g (5 oz) whole,
  unpeeled almonds
4 tablespoons brown
  sugar
1 teaspoon saffron
  threads*, soaked in
  3 tablespoons
  boiling water

Prick the lamb all over with a fork
and make about 12 deep cuts.

Blend the ginger, garlic, lemon
rind and juice, spices and salt in an
electric blender or food processor.
Spread over the lamb and leave to
stand for 1 hour in a flameproof
casserole.

Blend 4 tablespoons of the yogurt
with the almonds and 2 tablespoons
of the sugar. Stir in the remaining
yogurt and pour over the lamb.
Cover tightly and leave for 48 hours
in the refrigerator.

Let the meat return to room
temperature. Sprinkle over the
remaining sugar and cook,
uncovered, in a preheated hot oven,
220°C (425°F), Gas Mark 7, for
30 minutes. Cover, lower the
temperature to 160°C (325°F), Gas
Mark 3, and cook for 3 hours, basting
occasionally. Sprinkle the saffron
water over the meat and cook for a
further 30 minutes or until very
tender.

Remove the meat from the pan,
wrap it in foil and keep warm. Skim
off the fat from the casserole and boil
the sauce until thick. Place the meat
on a dish and pour over the sauce.
Carve in thick slices to serve.
Serves 6

Pork Vindaloo

1-2 teaspoons chilli
  powder*
1 teaspoon turmeric*
2 teaspoons ground
  cumin seeds*
2 teaspoons ground
  mustard seed*
2 tablespoons ground
  coriander seeds*
3.5 cm (1½ inch)
  piece ginger*,
  finely chopped
salt
150 ml (¼ pint)
  vinegar
1 large onion, finely
  chopped
2 cloves garlic,
  crushed
750 g (1½ lb) pork
  fillet, cubed
4 tablespoons oil

Mix the spices, and salt to taste with
the vinegar. Put the onion, garlic and
pork in a bowl, pour over the vinegar
mixture, cover and leave in the
refrigerator overnight.

Heat the oil in a large saucepan,
add the pork mixture, bring to
simmering point, cover and cook for
about 45 minutes or until the pork is
tender.

Serves 4

Hurry Curry

500 g (1 lb) stewing
  beef, lamb or pork,
  cubed
500 g (1 lb) onions,
  finely chopped
2.5 cm (1 inch) piece
  cinnamon stick*
6 cloves
1 tablespoon ground
  coriander seeds*
1 teaspoon ground
  cumin seeds*
½ teaspoon turmeric*
1 teaspoon chilli
  powder*
2.5 cm (1 inch) piece
  ginger*, finely
  chopped
1 tablespoon tomato
  purée
3 tablespoons oil
salt
250 g (8 oz) small
  new potatoes
  (optional)

Put all the ingredients except the
potatoes in a saucepan, seasoning
with salt to taste. Stir well. The
mixture should be moist; add an extra
tablespoon of oil if necessary. Cover
the pan tightly and leave overnight in
the refrigerator.

Cook over a moderately high heat
until the mixture starts to fry briskly.
Stir well, then lower the heat and
simmer for about 1½ hours or until
the meat is tender.

Add the potatoes, if using, about
20 minutes before the end of the
cooking time.
Serves 4

Pork Kebab

4 cloves garlic,
  chopped
10 cardamom*,
  peeled
1 teaspoon cumin
  seeds*
juice of 3 lemons
1 teaspoon chilli
  powder*
1 teaspoon garam
  masala*
1 tablespoon oil
1 teaspoon salt
750 g (1½ lb) pork
  fillet, cubed
2 tablespoons finely
  chopped coriander*
  to garnish

Place the garlic, cardamom, cumin
and lemon juice in an electric blender
or food processor and work to a
paste. Add the chilli powder, garam
masala, oil and salt and mix well.
Pour over the meat, stirring well so
that the cubes are thoroughly
covered. Cover and leave in the
refrigerator for 6 hours. Rub 4
skewers with oil, thread the meat on
them and cook under a preheated
moderate grill for 10 minutes, until
cooked through, turning the skewers
several times. Garnish with the
coriander to serve.
Serves 4

Bhuna Ghosht

750 g (1½ lb) pork
    fillets
2 tablespoons
    coriander seeds*,
    roughly pounded
1 teaspoon pepper
1 tablespoon paprika
salt
4 tablespoons oil
TO GARNISH:
2 tablespoons finely
    chopped coriander*
lemon wedges

Slit the fillets lengthways and cut each side into quarters. Prick them all over with a fork. Mix together the coriander, pepper, paprika, and salt to taste and rub into the meat on both sides. Leave to stand for 1 hour.

Heat the oil in a pan, add the meat and fry quickly on both sides to seal. Lower the heat and sauté for 5 minutes or until cooked through, stirring and turning to prevent burning.

Sprinkle with the coriander and serve with lemon.

Serves 4

Stuffed Cabbage Leaves

1 cabbage
5 tablespoons oil
1 onion, chopped
1 cm (½ inch) piece
    ginger*, chopped
1 teaspoon turmeric*
500 g (1 lb) lean
    minced lamb
75 g (3 oz) long-
    grain rice
2 tomatoes, skinned
    and chopped
grated rind and juice
    of 2 lemons
2 teaspoons sugar
salt and pepper
150 ml (¼ pint)
    water

Hollow out the stem end of the cabbage with a sharp knife. Place in a large pan, cover with water and bring to the boil. Remove from the heat, cover and leave for 15 minutes. Drain.

Heat 2 tablespoons of the oil in a pan, add the onion and fry until soft. Add the ginger and turmeric and fry gently for 1 minute. Add the lamb and fry briefly until brown. Cool slightly, then mix with the remaining ingredients, seasoning to taste.

Carefully remove 12 inner leaves of the cabbage. Divide the meat mixture between the 12 leaves, gently squeezing out and reserving any liquid. Fold each leaf into a packet.

Heat the remaining oil in a large lidded frying pan. Add the cabbage rolls in one layer as close together as possible; heat through. Pour on the reserved liquid and water. Bring to simmering point, cover and cook for about 30 minutes.

If the liquid has not evaporated, increase heat and cook uncovered for a few minutes. Lower heat, turn the rolls, cover and cook for 5 minutes.

Serves 4 to 6

POULTRY DISHES

Kashmiri Chicken

125 g (4 oz) butter
3 large onions, finely
  sliced
10 peppercorns
10 cardamom*
5 cm (2 inch) piece
  cinnamon stick
5 cm (2 inch) piece
  ginger*, chopped
2 cloves garlic, finely
  chopped
1 teaspoon chilli
  powder*
2 teaspoons paprika
salt
1.5 kg (3 lb) chicken
  pieces, skinned
250 g (8 oz) natural
  yogurt

Melt the butter in a deep, lidded
frying pan. Add the onions,
peppercorns, cardamom and
cinnamon and fry until the onions are
golden. Add the ginger, garlic, chilli
powder, paprika and salt to taste and
fry for 2 minutes, stirring
occasionally. Add the chicken pieces
and fry until browned. Gradually add
the yogurt, stirring constantly. Cover
and cook gently for about 30 minutes.
Serves 6

Chicken Curry

2 cloves garlic,
    chopped
5 cm (2 inch) piece
    ginger*, chopped
1 teaspoon turmeric*
2 teaspoons cumin
    seeds*, ground
1 teaspoon chilli
    powder*
1 teaspoon pepper
3 tablespoons finely
    chopped coriander*
500 g (1 lb) natural
    yogurt
salt
1 kg (2 lb) chicken
    pieces, skinned
4 tablespoons oil
2 onions, chopped

Place the garlic, ginger, turmeric, cumin, chilli, pepper, coriander, yogurt and salt to taste in a large bowl. Mix well, add the chicken and leave for 4 hours, turning occasionally.

Heat the oil in a pan, add the onion and fry until golden. Add the chicken and the marinade. Bring to simmering point, cover and cook for about 30 minutes, until the chicken is tender.

Serves 4

Palak Murg

3 tablespoons oil
2 onions, chopped
2 cloves garlic, crushed
2.5 cm (1 inch) piece
    ginger*, chopped
2 teaspoons ground
    coriander seeds*
1 teaspoon chilli
    powder*
salt
750 g (1½ lb)
    chicken legs and
    thighs, skinned
750 g (1½ lb) spinach
milk (optional)

Heat the oil in a large saucepan, add the onions and fry until golden. Add the garlic, ginger, coriander, chilli powder, and salt to taste and fry gently for 2 minutes, stirring.

Add the chicken and fry on all sides until browned. Add the spinach, stir well, cover and simmer for 35 minutes, until the chicken is tender.

If the mixture becomes too dry during cooking, add 2 to 3 tablespoons milk. If there is too much liquid left at the end, uncover and cook for a few minutes until evaporated.

Serves 4

Chicken Korma

2 onions
2 cloves garlic
2.5 cm (1 inch) piece
    ginger*, chopped
2 green chillies*,
    chopped
1 tablespoon
    coriander seeds*
1 teaspoon salt
2 tablespoons water
50 g (2 oz) almonds
750 g (1½ lb) chicken
    pieces, skinned
3 tablespoons oil
6 cardamom*
6 cloves
2.5 cm (1 inch) piece
    cinnamon stick*
150 g (5.2 oz)
    natural yogurt
142 ml (5 fl oz)
    single cream
¼ teaspoon powdered
    saffron*, soaked in
    1 tablespoon warm
    water
2 tablespoons
    chopped coriander*

Chop one onion and place in an electric blender or food processor with the garlic, ginger, chillies, coriander seeds, salt, water and half the almonds and blend until smooth. Spoon the mixture over the chicken pieces, mix well and set aside for 1 hour.

Finely chop the second onion. Heat the oil in a pan, add the onion, cardamom, cloves and cinnamon and fry until the onion is soft. Add the chicken and marinade and fry, stirring, until dry.

Add the yogurt, a tablespoon at a time, stirring until absorbed. Cover and simmer very gently for 30 minutes, adding a little water if necessary.

Place the remaining almonds, the cream and saffron in the electric blender or food processor and blend until smooth. Stir into the chicken, check the seasoning, cover and simmer for about 5 more minutes, until the chicken is tender.

Sprinkle with coriander to serve.

Serves 4

Hamicabab

2 tablespoons oil
2 cloves garlic, finely
   chopped
1 teaspoon turmeric*
1 kg (2 lb) chicken
   pieces
250 g (8 oz)
   potatoes, cut into
   large cubes
250 g (8 oz) shallots
salt and pepper

Heat the oil in a deep, lidded frying pan. Add the garlic and turmeric and fry for 1 minute, being careful to avoid burning. Add the chicken pieces and fry for about 10 minutes, until well browned.

Add the potatoes and shallots and fry for 2 minutes. Add salt and pepper to taste and just enough water to cover the bottom of the pan. Cover and simmer gently for about 25 minutes or until tender, adding water if necessary to prevent burning.

Uncover the pan and leave on the heat for a few minutes, until all the liquid has evaporated.
Serves 4

Chicken and Dhal Curry

250 g (8 oz) masoor
   dhal*
600 ml (1 pint) water
salt
3 tablespoons oil
2 onions, minced
2 cloves garlic,
   minced
2.5 cm (1 inch) piece
   ginger*, minced
1 tablespoon ground
   coriander seeds*
1 teaspoon ground
   cumin seeds*
½ teaspoon turmeric*
½ teaspoon ground
   cloves
2 teaspoons chilli
   powder*
750 g (1½ lb)
   chicken thighs

Wash the dhal, soak in clean water for
1 hour, then drain and boil in the
water with 1 teaspoon salt added, for
about 1 hour, until soft. Drain and set
aside.

Heat the oil in a saucepan, add the
onion, garlic and ginger and fry for
about 5 minutes. Add the spices and
salt to taste and fry gently for 10
minutes; if the mixture becomes too
dry, add 2 tablespoons water. Add
the chicken and fry until golden all
over. Add the cooked dhal, cover and
simmer for about 30 minutes, or until
the chicken is tender.

Serves 4

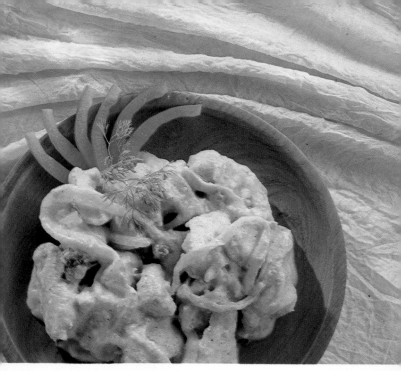

Chicken Molee

about 3 tablespoons oil
4 chicken breasts,
    skinned and boned,
    cut into 3 or 4 pieces
6 cardamom*
6 cloves
5 cm (2 inch) piece
    cinnamon stick*
1 large onion, finely
    sliced
2 cloves garlic
3.5 cm (1½ inch)
    piece ginger*,
    chopped
3 green chillies*,
    seeded
juice of 1 lemon
1 teaspoon turmeric*
50 g (2 oz) creamed
    coconut*
150 ml (¼ pint) hot
    water
· salt

Heat the oil in a pan, add the chicken and fry quickly all over. Remove with a slotted spoon and set aside.

Add a little more oil to the pan if necessary and fry the cardamom, cloves and cinnamon for 1 minute. Add the onion and fry until soft.

Place the garlic, ginger, chillies and lemon juice in an electric blender or food processor and work to a smooth paste. Add to the pan with the turmeric and cook for 5 minutes.

Melt the coconut in the hot water and add to the pan with salt to taste. Simmer for 2 minutes, then add the chicken pieces and any juices. Simmer for 15 to 20 minutes, until tender.

Serves 4

47

Tandoori Chicken

½-1 teaspoon chilli
  powder*
1 teaspoon pepper
1 teaspoon salt
2 tablespoons lemon
  juice
1 × 1.5 kg (3 lb)
  oven-ready
  chicken, skinned
4 tablespoons natural
  yogurt
3 cloves garlic
5 cm (2 inch) piece
  ginger*
2 small dried red
  chillies*
1 tablespoon
  coriander seeds*
2 teaspoons cumin
  seeds*
50 g (2 oz) butter,
  melted

Mix the chilli powder, pepper, salt
and lemon juice together. Slash the
chicken all over and rub the mixture
into the cuts. Set aside for 1 hour.

Place the yogurt, garlic, ginger,
chillies, coriander and cumin in an
electric blender or food processor and
work to a paste. Spread it all over the
chicken. Cover and leave in the
refrigerator overnight. Return to
room temperature before cooking.

Place on a rack in a roasting pan
and pour over half the butter. Cook
in a preheated moderately hot oven,
200°C (400°F), Gas Mark 6, for 1 hour
or until tender. Baste occasionally and
pour on the remaining butter halfway
through cooking time.

Serves 4

NOTES: If preferred, the chicken can be
spit-roasted for about 1 hour, using
all the butter at the start.

The typical red colour of tandoori
chicken is from a food colouring which
is obtainable from Asian food shops.
It has been omitted from this recipe,
because many people are allergic to it.

Murgh Mussalam

2 onions
2 cloves garlic
5 cm (2 inch) piece
  ginger*
1 teaspoon poppy
  seeds
8 peppercorns
2 × 150 g (5.2 oz)
  cartons natural
  yogurt
1 teaspoon garam
  masala*
salt
1 × 1.5 kg (3 lb)
  oven-ready chicken
125 g (4 oz) long-
  grain rice, soaked
  in cold water for
  1 hour
3 tablespoons ghee*
½ teaspoon chilli
  powder*
50 g (2 oz) sultanas
50 g (2 oz) slivered
  almonds
350 ml (12 fl oz)
  water

Place the onions, garlic, ginger, poppy seeds, peppercorns and half the yogurt in an electric blender or food processor and work to a paste. Stir in the garam masala, add salt to taste.

Prick the chicken all over with a fork and rub in the blended mixture. Leave for 1 hour. Drain the rice.

Heat 1 tablespoon of the ghee in a pan, add the rice and fry for 3 minutes, stirring constantly. Add the chilli powder, sultanas, almonds and salt to taste and stir well. Pour in 175 ml (6 fl oz) of the water, cover and simmer for about 10 minutes, until the rice is almost tender; cool.

When the rice is cold, use it to stuff the chicken; sew up both ends. Heat the remaining ghee or oil in a pan and add the chicken, on its side. Pour in any marinade and the remaining water. Bring to simmering point, cover and cook for 1 hour, turning over halfway through cooking time.

Add the remaining yogurt, a spoonful at a time, stirring until it is all absorbed. Add more salt if necessary. Cook for a further 15 minutes, until the chicken is tender.
Serves 4

FISH DISHES

Fish Molee

750 g (1½ lb) cod
   fillet, skinned
2 tablespoons flour
4 tablespoons oil
2 onions, sliced
2 cloves garlic, crushed
1 teaspoon turmeric*
4 green chillies*,
   finely chopped
2 tablespoons lemon
   juice
175 ml (6 fl oz) thick
   coconut milk*
salt

Cut the fish into 4 pieces and coat with the flour. Heat the oil in a frying pan, add the fish and fry quickly on both sides. Remove with a slotted spoon and set aside.

Add the onion and garlic to the pan and fry until soft and golden. Add the turmeric, chillies, lemon juice, coconut milk, and salt to taste and simmer, uncovered, for 10 minutes or until thickened.

Add the fish and any juices, spoon over the sauce and cook gently for 2 to 3 minutes, until tender.
Serves 4

Baked Spiced Fish

4 tablespoons oil
125 g (4 oz) grated
  coconut*
5 cm (2 inch) piece
  ginger*, chopped
1 large onion,
  chopped
4 cloves garlic, finely
  chopped
2 green chillies*,
  seeded and chopped
1 teaspoon chilli
  powder*
2 tablespoons finely
  chopped coriander*
4 tablespoons lemon
  juice
salt
1 kg (2 lb) cod steaks

Heat the oil in a pan, add the coconut, ginger, onion, garlic, chillies and chilli powder and fry gently until the onion is translucent. Add the coriander, lemon juice and salt to taste and simmer for 15 minutes or until the coconut is soft.

Oil the bottom of a baking dish just large enough to hold the fish. Arrange the fish steaks side by side and pour over the spice mixture.

Bake in a preheated moderate oven, 160°C (325°F), Gas Mark 3, for 25 minutes or until tender.
Serves 4

Prawn Kebab

2 tablespoons oil
1 tablespoon lemon
juice
2 cloves garlic,
crushed
1 teaspoon paprika
1/2 teaspoon chilli
powder*
1/2 teaspoon salt
1/2 teaspoon turmeric*
1 tablespoon finely
chopped coriander*
12 giant Pacific
prawns, shelled

Place all the ingredients in a shallow dish, stirring to coat the prawns thoroughly. Cover and chill for several hours, stirring occasionally.

Thread the prawns on skewers, or place in the grill pan, and cook under a preheated moderate grill for 3 to 4 minutes on each side, or until cooked. Spoon over the pan juices when turning.
Serves 4

Prawn Chilli Fry

3 tablespoons oil
3 onions, sliced
2 green chillies*,
chopped
2.5 cm (1 inch) piece
ginger*, chopped
1/2 teaspoon chilli
powder*
1/2 teaspoon turmeric*
salt
227 g (8 oz) frozen
prawns -

Heat the oil in a pan, add the onions and fry until soft and golden. Add the chillies, ginger, chilli powder, turmeric and salt to taste and fry for 2 minutes.

Add the prawns and cook, uncovered, for about 3 minutes or until all the moisture has evaporated.

This is very good served with dhal (see page 64) and rice.
Serves 4

Bombay Fish Curry

2 tablespoons oil
2 tablespoons finely
chopped onion
2 cloves garlic, crushed
1 tablespoon finely
chopped ginger*
1/2 teaspoon chilli
powder*
4 green chillies*
300 ml (1/2 pint) thin
coconut milk*
salt
4 fish cutlets (halibut,
cod, etc.)

Heat the oil in a pan, add the onion, garlic, ginger and chilli powder and fry until the onion is soft. Add the chillies, coconut milk and salt to taste and simmer until thickened. Add the fish, spooning the sauce over, and cook, uncovered, for about 5 minutes or until tender.
Serves 4

Amotik

50 g (2 oz)
  tamarind*, soaked
  in 6 tablespoons
  hot water for
  30 minutes
4 tablespoons oil
750 g (1½ lb)
  monkfish or other
  firm white fish,
  cubed
flour for dusting
1 onion, chopped
4 green chillies*,
  finely chopped
2 cloves garlic,
  crushed
1 teaspoon ground
  cumin seeds*
½-1 teaspoon chilli
  powder*
salt
1 tablespoon vinegar

Strain the tamarind, squeezing out as much water as possible. Discard the tamarind and reserve the water.

Heat the oil in a large pan. Lightly dust the fish with flour, add to the pan and fry quickly on both sides. Remove from the pan with a slotted spoon and set aside.

Add the onion to the pan and fry until soft and golden. Add the tamarind water, chillies, garlic, cumin, chilli powder, and salt to taste and cook for 10 minutes. Add the fish and any juices and the vinegar. Simmer, uncovered, for about 5 minutes; be careful not to overcook.
Serves 4

Grilled Spiced Fish

2 large or 4 small
 plaice, cleaned
150 g (5.2 oz)
 natural yogurt
2 cloves garlic,
 crushed
1 teaspoon ground
 coriander seeds*
1/2 teaspoon chilli
 powder*
1 teaspoon garam
 masala*
1 tablespoon vinegar
 or lemon juice
1 tablespoon oil
salt
TO GARNISH:
2 tablespoons finely
 chopped parsley
1 lemon, quartered

Slash the fish on both sides and place in separate shallow dishes. Mix the remaining ingredients together, adding salt to taste, and divide between the fish. Spoon it all over one side and leave for 1 hour, then turn and spoon over the juice that has collected in the dish. Leave for another hour.

Cook under a preheated moderate grill for 3 to 4 minutes. Turn and baste with any juices collected in the grill pan, then cook for a further 3 or 4 minutes.

Serve sprinkled with the parsley and accompanied by lemon quarters.
Serves 4

Masala Machi

4 herrings or
    mackerel, boned
    and cleaned
1 teaspoon salt
2 tablespoons lemon
    juice
2 cloves garlic
4 green chillies*,
    seeded
4 tablespoons
    coriander leaves*
1 teaspoon ground
    coriander seeds*
3 tablespoons oil
1 onion, chopped
lemon wedges to
    garnish

Slash the fish, sprinkle a little salt inside each one and set aside.

Place the lemon juice, garlic, chillies, coriander leaves and seeds and remaining salt in an electric blender or food processor and work to a paste.

Heat 2 tablespoons oil in a pan, add the onions and fry until golden. Add the blended spices and fry gently, stirring, for 5 minutes, until the mixture is thick and smooth.

Spread the paste inside each fish and brush lightly with the remaining oil.

Cook under a preheated moderate grill for about 4 minutes on each side. Or wrap in foil and cook in a preheated moderate oven, 180°C (350°F), Gas Mark 4, for about 20 minutes, until tender.

Garnish with lemon wedges to serve.
Serves 4

Prawn and Egg Curry

4 tablespoons oil
1 large onion, chopped
1 clove garlic, chopped
2.5 cm (1 inch) piece
    ginger*, chopped
1 tablespoon ground
    coriander seeds*
2 teaspoons ground
    cumin seeds*
1 teaspoon chilli
    powder*
1 tablespoon tomato
    purée
300 ml (½ pint) water
salt
6 hard-boiled eggs,
    halved
227 g (8 oz) frozen
    prawns
25 g (1 oz) creamed
    coconut*

Heat the oil in a saucepan, add the onion and fry until golden. Add the garlic and ginger and fry for 1 minute. Add the remaining spices and fry gently for 2 minutes, stirring occasionally; if the mixture becomes too dry, add 1 tablespoon water. Add the tomato purée, mix well, then add the water and salt to taste. Cover and simmer for 10 minutes.

Add the eggs, spooning some mixture over them, cover and cook for 15 minutes, stirring occasionally.

Stir in the prawns. When the curry starts to simmer again, stir in the creamed coconut. Let the mixture come to simmering point once more, then serve immediately.
Serves 4

Fish Fritters

6 tablespoons oil
2 onions, chopped
1 tablespoon ground
  coriander seeds*
3 green chillies*,
  seeded and chopped
1 teaspoon salt
1 teaspoon pepper
750 g (1½ lb) cod
  fillets, skinned and
  cut into small
  pieces
2 tablespoons finely
  chopped coriander*
BATTER:
125 g (4 oz) gram
  flour*
½ teaspoon chilli
  powder*
½ teaspoon salt
1 egg, beaten
7 tablespoons water

Heat 3 tablespoons of the oil in a pan, add the onion and fry until just soft. Stir in the coriander, chillies, salt and pepper, then add the fish. Fry for 2 minutes, then cover and cook on very low heat for 2 minutes. Break up the mixture with a fork and add the chopped coriander. Remove from the heat and set aside while making the batter.

Sift the flour, chilli powder and salt into a bowl. Add the egg and water and beat well to make a smooth batter. Leave to stand for 30 minutes, then stir in the fish mixture.

Heat the remaining oil in a frying pan and drop in small spoonfuls of the batter mixture. Fry on both sides until golden. Drain thoroughly and keep warm while frying the remainder.
Serves 4

Pickled Haddock Steaks

4 tablespoons oil
4 haddock steaks, each
    weighing about
    250 g (8 oz),
    cleaned
2 onions, chopped
2 cloves garlic
2.5 cm (1 inch) piece
    ginger*
1 tablespoon
    coriander seeds*
4 green chillies*,
    seeded
5 tablespoons vinegar
1/2 teaspoon turmeric*
4 curry leaves*
salt

Heat the oil in a large frying pan, add the fish and fry on both sides until browned. Remove with a slotted spoon and set aside. Add the onions to the pan and fry until soft.

Place the garlic, ginger, coriander seeds, chillies and 1 tablespoon of the vinegar in an electric blender or food processor and work to a paste. Add to the pan with the turmeric, curry leaves, and salt to taste and fry for 3 to 4 minutes.

Add the remaining vinegar, bring to simmering point, stir well and add the fish. Cook, uncovered, for 3 to 4 minutes, until tender.

Place the fish in a dish, pour over all the juices and leave to cool. Cover and keep in the refrigerator for at least 12 hours. Serve cold.
Serves 4

VEGETABLE DISHES

Spicy Turnips

about 3 tablespoons
  ghee*
1 kg (2 lb) turnips,
  quartered
2 cloves garlic
2 green chillies*
2.5 cm (1 inch) piece
  ginger*
1 teaspoon cumin
  seeds*
2 teaspoons coriander
  seeds*
2 tablespoons natural
  yogurt
1 teaspoon salt
150ml (¼pint) water
1 teaspoon sugar
1 teaspoon garam
  masala*

Heat the ghee in a pan, add the
turnips and fry lightly; set aside.

Place the garlic, chillies, ginger,
cumin, coriander and yogurt in an
electric blender or food processor and
work to a paste. Add to the pan,
adding more ghee if necessary, and
fry for 2 minutes.

Return the turnips to the pan, add
the salt and stir well. Add the water
and simmer, covered, for about
10 minutes, until almost tender.
Uncover the pan, add the sugar and
garam masala and cook briskly,
stirring, until most of the liquid has
evaporated.
Serves 4 to 6

Tomato and Coriander

3 tablespoons oil or
    ghee*
2 onions, chopped
1 kg (2 lb) tomatoes,
    sliced
2.5 cm (1 inch) piece
    ginger*, chopped
1 teaspoon ground
    cumin seeds*
1 teaspoon ground
    coriander seeds*
½ teaspoon chilli
    powder*
1 teaspoon salt
3 green chillies*
1 teaspoon sugar
50 g (2 oz) coriander*,
    finely chopped

Heat the oil or ghee in a pan, add the
onions and fry until soft. Add the
tomatoes, ginger, cumin, coriander,
chilli powder, and salt and simmer,
uncovered, until the mixture begins
to thicken. Add the chillies and sugar
and continue cooking for 5 to
10 minutes, until fairly thick. Stir in
the coriander and serve.
Serves 4

Phul Gobi with Peppers

3 tablespoons oil
1 onion, sliced
½ teaspoon turmeric*
1 cauliflower, broken
    into florets
salt
2 green chillies*,
    seeded
1 green, 1 yellow and
    1 red pepper,
    cored, seeded and
    cut into strips

Heat the oil in a pan, add the onion and fry until soft. Add the turmeric and cook for 1 minute. Add the cauliflower and salt to taste, stir well, cover and cook gently for about 10 minutes, until the cauliflower is almost cooked.

Add the chillies and peppers, stir and cook for a further 5 minutes or until tender.

Serves 4

Aloo Mattar

5 tablespoons oil
1 onion, chopped
2.5 cm (1 inch) piece
    ginger*, chopped
1 green chilli*, finely
    chopped
2 cloves garlic, crushed
1 teaspoon turmeric*
750 g (1½ lb)
    potatoes, cut into
    small cubes
salt
6-8 mint leaves
250 g (8 oz) shelled
    or frozen peas

Heat the oil in a pan, add the onion and fry until soft and translucent. Add the ginger, chilli, garlic and turmeric, stir well and cook for 5 minutes. Add the potatoes and salt to taste, stir well, cover and cook for 5 minutes.

Add the mint and fresh peas, stir well and cook for 20 minutes, until tender. If using frozen peas, add them after the potatoes have cooked for 15 minutes and cook for 3 minutes only.

Serves 4 to 6

Gobi ki Foogath

3 tablespoons oil
1 onion, finely sliced
2 cloves garlic, crushed
3 green chillies*,
    seeded and finely
    chopped
2.5 cm (1 inch) piece
    ginger*, finely
    chopped
500 g (1 lb) white
    cabbage, finely
    sliced
salt

Heat the oil in a large pan, add the onion and fry until just soft. Add the garlic, chillies and ginger and cook for 1 minute. Add the cabbage, with the water clinging to the leaves after washing, and salt to taste. Stir very well, cover and cook, stirring occasionally, for about 15 minutes; the cabbage should still be slightly crunchy. If liquid gathers, uncover the pan for the last 5 minutes to allow it to evaporate.

Serves 4

Masoor Dhal

4 tablespoons oil
6 cloves
6 cardamom*
2.5 cm (1 inch) piece
  cinnamon stick*
1 onion, chopped
2.5 cm (1 inch) piece
  ginger*, chopped
1 green chilli*, finely
  chopped
1 clove garlic,
  chopped
1/2 teaspoon garam
  masala*
250 g (8 oz) masoor
  dhal*
salt
juice of 1 lemon

Heat the oil in a pan, add the cloves,
cardamom and cinnamon and fry
until they start to swell. Add the
onion and fry until translucent. Add
ginger, chilli, garlic and garam
masala and cook for about 5 minutes.

Add the lentils, stir thoroughly
and fry for 1 minute. Add salt to taste
and enough water to come about 3 cm
(1¼ inches) above the level of the
lentils. Bring to the boil, cover and
simmer for about 20 minutes, until
really thick and tender.

Sprinkle with the lemon juice, stir
and serve immediately.
Serves 4

Panir Mattar

125 g (4 oz) panir*
2-3 tablespoons oil
2 tablespoons finely
  chopped onion
90 ml (3 fl oz) water
salt
250 g (8 oz) shelled
  peas
1/2 teaspoon sugar
1 tablespoon grated
  ginger*
2 green chillies*,
  finely chopped
1/2 teaspoon garam
  masala*
1 tablespoon finely
  chopped coriander*

Cut the panir into 1 cm (1/2 inch)
cubes. Heat the oil in a heavy-based
pan, add the panir and fry until
golden, turning gently and taking
care not to burn. Remove from the
pan and set aside. Add the onions to
the pan and fry until coloured;
remove and set aside.

Add the water, and salt to taste, to
the pan and bring to the boil. Add the
peas and sugar, cover and simmer
until the peas are almost tender. If
necessary, uncover and cook for
1 minute to evaporate any liquid.

Add the onions, ginger and chillies
and stir well. Cook for 2 minutes,
then very gently stir in the panir.
Heat through for 2 minutes, then stir
in the garam masala and coriander.
Serve immediately.
Serves 4

Sprouting Mung Dhal

250 g (8 oz) whole
   mung beans, rinsed
3-4 tablespoons oil
1 onion, thinly sliced
2 green chillies*,
   seeded and chopped
2.5 cm (1 inch) piece
   ginger*, cut into
   fine matchsticks
1 teaspoon fennel
   seeds*
salt
300 ml (½ pint)
   water

A day in advance, put the beans in a bowl and barely cover them with warm water. Cover the bowl with cling wrap and leave in a warm dark place. Do not let the beans dry out; add a little extra water if necessary. The beans will have sprouted by the next day. Rinse and drain them.

Heat the oil in a saucepan. Add the onion and fry, stirring, for 3 minutes. Stir in the chillies, ginger, and fennel seeds and cook, stirring, until the onions have softened a little.

Add the beans, salt to taste and the water. Bring to simmering point, cover and cook gently, stirring occasionally, for 25 to 30 minutes or until the beans are soft and there is no liquid left.

Serves 4

Courgette, Peas and Coriander

4 tablespoons oil
2 onions, sliced
2 cloves garlic, finely
   chopped
2 green chillies*,
   chopped
2.5 cm (1 inch) piece
   ginger*, chopped
4 tablespoons finely
   chopped coriander*
salt
500 g (1 lb)
   courgettes, cut into
   5 mm (¼ inch)
   slices
250 g (8 oz) shelled
   peas

Heat the oil in a pan, add the onion and fry until soft. Add the garlic, chillies, ginger, coriander and salt to taste and cook for 5 minutes, stirring occasionally. Add the courgettes and peas, stir well, cover and cook for 30 minutes, or until the peas are tender. If necessary, boil quickly to evaporate any liquid before serving.

Serves 4

Aloo Sag

6 tablespoons oil
1 onion, chopped
2.5 cm (1 inch) piece
  ginger*, chopped
2 green chillies*,
  finely chopped
1 teaspoon turmeric*
2 cloves garlic, finely
  chopped
500 g (1 lb) potatoes,
  cut into small pieces
salt
2 × 227 g (8 oz)
  packets frozen
  spinach leaf,
  thawed

Heat the oil in a lidded frying pan,
add the onion and cook until soft.
Add the spices and garlic and cook for
5 minutes. Add the potatoes, and salt
to taste, stir well, cover and cook for
10 minutes.
  Squeeze out any liquid from the
spinach and chop. Add to the
potatoes and cook for about
5 minutes, until both vegetables are
tender.
Serves 4

Tamatar Aloo

2 tablespoons oil
1/2 teaspoon mustard
    seeds*
250 g (8 oz)
    potatoes, cut into
    small cubes
1 teaspoon turmeric*
1 teaspoon chilli
    powder*
2 teaspoons paprika
juice of 1 lemon
1 teaspoon sugar
salt
250 g (8 oz) tomatoes,
    quartered
2 tablespoons finely
    chopped coriander*
    to garnish

Heat the oil in a pan, add the mustard
seeds and fry until they pop – just a
few seconds. Add the potatoes and
fry for about 5 minutes. Add the
spices, lemon juice, sugar and salt
to taste, stir well and cook for
5 minutes.

Add the tomatoes, stir well, then
simmer for 5 to 10 minutes until the
potatoes are tender.

Sprinkle with coriander to serve.
Serves 4

Dhai Aloo

4 tablespoons oil
1 onion, chopped
2.5 cm (1 inch) piece
  ginger*, finely
  chopped
1 tablespoon ground
  coriander seeds*
2 green chillies*,
  finely chopped
750 g (1½ lb) small
  new potatoes
1 × 227 g (8 oz) can
  tomatoes
100 g (3½ oz) raisins
salt
2 × 150 g (5.2 oz)
  cartons natural
  yogurt
2 tablespoons chopped
  coriander* to
  garnish

Heat the oil in a large pan, add the
onion and ginger and fry until soft.
Stir in the coriander seeds and chillies
and fry for 2 minutes. Add the
potatoes, stir well, cover and cook
very gently for 5 minutes, stirring
occasionally so they colour evenly.

Add the tomatoes with their juice,
raisins and salt to taste and stir well.
Increase the heat a little and cook,
uncovered. As the liquid evaporates,
add half the yogurt, a tablespoon at a
time. When the potatoes have cooked
for 20 minutes and are just about
ready, add the remaining yogurt, a
tablespoon at a time, lower the heat
and cook for 2 minutes. Sprinkle with
coriander to serve.

Serves 4 to 6

Potato with Mustard Seed

4 tablespoons oil
1 teaspoon mustard
  seeds*
1 teaspoon turmeric*
1-2 green chillies*,
  chopped
500 g (1 lb) potatoes,
  boiled and diced
juice of 1 lemon
salt

Heat the oil in a frying pan and add the mustard seeds. When they begin to pop, stir in the turmeric and chillies and cook for a few seconds. Add the potatoes and stir well to mix. Pour in the lemon juice and add salt to taste. Stir well and heat through.
Serves 4

Bharta

500 g (1 lb)
  aubergines
2 tablespoons oil
1 large onion, finely
  chopped
1 clove garlic, crushed
1 green chilli*, seeded
  and chopped
1 tablespoon ground
  coriander seeds*
1 tablespoon finely
  chopped coriander*
salt
1 tablespoon lemon
  juice

Cook the aubergines in a preheated moderate oven, 180°C (350°F), Gas Mark 4, for 30 minutes or until soft. Cool slightly, then slit open, scoop out all the flesh and beat it with a fork.

Heat the oil in a pan, add the onion, garlic and chilli and fry until the onion is soft but not coloured. Add the ground and fresh coriander and salt to taste. Add the aubergine pulp, stir well and fry, uncovered, for 2 minutes, then cover and simmer very gently for 5 minutes. Sprinkle with lemon juice and serve.
Serves 4

Dhai Bhindi

250 g (8 oz) okra
2 tablespoons oil
2.5 cm (1 inch) piece
  ginger*, chopped
1 teaspoon turmeric*
salt
2-3 tablespoons water
2 × 150 g (5.2 oz)
  cartons natural
  yogurt
1/2 teaspoon chilli
  powder*
2 tablespoons grated
  coconut*
1 tablespoon finely
  chopped coriander*

Cut the tops off the okra and halve them lengthways. Heat the oil in a pan, add the okra and fry for 5 minutes. Add the ginger, turmeric, and salt to taste, stir well, add the water, cover and cook for 10 minutes, until the okra is tender.

Mix the remaining ingredients together; add to the pan, stir well and serve.
Serves 4

71

Kabli Channa

250 g (8 oz) whole
  Bengal gram*
750 ml (1¼ pints)
  water
1 teaspoon salt
2 tablespoons ghee*
  or oil
1 onion, chopped
2.5 cm (1 inch) piece
  cinnamon stick*
4 cloves
2 cloves garlic,
  crushed
2.5 cm (1 inch) piece
  ginger*, chopped
2 green chillies*,
  finely chopped
2 teaspoons ground
  coriander seeds
150 g (5 oz)
  tomatoes, chopped
1 teaspoon garam
  masala*
1 tablespoon finely
  chopped coriander*

Wash the gram and soak in the water overnight. Add the salt and simmer until tender. Drain, reserving the water, and set aside.

Heat the ghee or oil in a pan, add the onion and fry until golden. Add the cinnamon and cloves and fry for a few seconds, then add the garlic, ginger, chillies and ground coriander and fry for 5 minutes. Add the tomatoes and fry until most of the liquid has evaporated.

Add the gram and cook gently for 5 minutes, then add the reserved water and simmer for 20 to 25 minutes. Add the garam masala and stir well. Sprinkle with the chopped coriander and serve immediately.
Serves 4

Vegetable Curry

3 tablespoons oil
1 teaspoon fennel
  seeds*
2 onions, sliced
1 teaspoon chilli
  powder*
1 tablespoon ground
  coriander seeds*
2.5 cm (1 inch) piece
  ginger*, chopped
salt
2 aubergines, sliced
175 g (6 oz) shelled
  peas
125 g (4 oz)
  potatoes, cubed
1 × 227 g (8 oz) can
  tomatoes
4 green chillies*

Heat the oil in a large pan, add the
fennel seeds and fry for a few
seconds, then add the onions and fry
until soft and golden. Add the chilli
powder, coriander, ginger and salt to
taste and fry for 2 minutes. Add the
aubergines, peas and potatoes and
cook for 5 minutes, stirring
occasionally.

  Add the tomatoes with their juice
and the chillies, cover and simmer
for 30 minutes, or until the peas are
tender and the sauce is thick.
Serves 4

RICE DISHES

Tomato Rice

250 g (8 oz) long-
    grain rice
3 tablespoons oil
1 onion, sliced
1 clove garlic, crushed
2.5 cm (1 inch) piece
    ginger*, chopped
1 × 539 g (1 lb 3 oz)
    can tomatoes
salt
2 tablespoons finely
    chopped coriander*

Wash the rice under running cold water, then soak in fresh cold water for 30 minutes; drain thoroughly.

Heat the oil in a large pan, add the onion and fry until golden. Add the garlic and ginger and fry for 2 minutes. Add the rice, stir well and fry for 2 minutes.

Break up the tomatoes in their juice and add to the rice with salt to taste. Bring to the boil, then cover and simmer for 15 to 20 minutes, until tender.

Transfer to a warmed serving dish and sprinkle with the coriander.
Serves 4

Kitcheri

175 g (6 oz) long-
   grain rice
175 g (6 oz) masoor
   dhal*
50 g (2 oz) butter
1 onion
1 clove garlic,
   chopped
5 cm (2 inch) piece
   cinnamon stick*
5 cardamom*
5 cloves
10 peppercorns
450 ml (¾ pint)
   boiling water
salt

Wash the combined rice and dhal under running cold water, then leave to soak in fresh cold water for 30 minutes.

Melt the butter in a large pan. Add the onion to the pan with the garlic, cinnamon, cardamom, cloves and peppercorns. Fry gently until the onion is soft.

Add the drained rice and dhal to the pan and fry gently, stirring, for 2 minutes. Add the water, and salt to taste and boil for 2 minutes. Cover tightly and simmer for about 20 minutes, until the water is absorbed.

Transfer the rice mixture to a warmed serving dish to serve.

Serves 4

NOTE: Kitcheri looks most attractive garnished with crisply fried onion rings.

Chicken Pilau

350 g (12 oz)
  Basmati rice
1 × 1.5 kg (3½ lb)
  oven-ready chicken
5 tablespoons ghee*
  or butter
5 cm (2 inch) piece
  cinnamon stick*
8 cloves
6 cardamom*
2 cloves garlic,
  crushed
½-1 teaspoon chilli
  powder*
1 tablespoon fennel
  seeds*
5 tablespoons natural
  yogurt
1 teaspoon powdered
  saffron*
1½ teaspoons salt
about 600 ml (1 pint)
  chicken stock
TO GARNISH:
4 tablespoons ghee*
  or butter
2 large onions, sliced

Wash the rice under cold water, then soak in fresh cold water for 30 minutes; drain thoroughly. Skin the chicken and cut into pieces.

Melt the ghee or butter in a large flameproof casserole. Add the cinnamon, cloves and cardamom and fry for 30 seconds. Stir in the garlic, chilli and fennel and fry for 30 seconds.

Add the chicken and fry, turning, for 5 minutes. Add the yogurt a spoonful at a time, stirring until absorbed before adding the next spoonful. Cover and simmer for 25 minutes or until tender.

Add the rice, saffron and salt. Fry, stirring, until the rice is well mixed and glistening. Add enough stock to cover the rice by 5 mm (¼ inch) and bring to the boil. Reduce the heat to very low, cover tightly and cook for 20 minutes or until the rice is cooked and the liquid absorbed.

Melt the ghee or butter in a small pan, add the onion and fry until golden. Transfer the pilau to a warmed dish, and garnish with the fried onion.
Serves 6

Boiled Rice

350 g (12 oz) long-
grain rice
450 ml (¾ pint)
water
salt

Wash the rice very thoroughly under running cold water, then soak in clean cold water for 30 minutes; drain.

Place in a large pan with the water and salt to taste and bring to the boil. Cover, turn down the heat to very low and cook for 20 to 25 minutes, until the rice is tender and the liquid absorbed.

Serves 4 to 6
Illustrated on pages 38 and 39

Prawn Pilau

350 g (12 oz)
Basmati rice
6 tablespoons ghee*
or butter
1 tablespoon
coriander seeds*,
crushed
½ teaspoon turmeric*
1 small pineapple,
cubed, or 1 × 227 g
(8 oz) can
pineapple cubes,
drained
227 g (8 oz) frozen
prawns, thawed
1 teaspoon salt
about 600 ml (1 pint)
fish or chicken
stock
TO GARNISH:
2 tablespoons ghee*
or butter
2 tablespoons
sultanas
2 tablespoons cashew
nuts
2 hard-boiled eggs,
quartered
2 tablespoons
chopped coriander*

Wash the rice under cold running water, then soak in fresh cold water for 30 minutes; drain thoroughly.

Melt the ghee or butter in a large saucepan, add the coriander seeds and fry for 30 seconds. Add the turmeric and stir for a few seconds, then add the pineapple and fry, stirring, for 30 seconds. Add the prawns, rice and salt. (If using a stock cube, omit the salt.) Fry, stirring, for 1 minute, then pour in enough stock to cover the rice by 5 mm (¼ inch). Bring to the boil, cover tightly and cook very gently for 25 minutes or until the rice is cooked and the liquid absorbed.

Meanwhile, prepare the garnish. Heat the ghee or butter in a small pan, add the sultanas and cashews and fry for 1 to 2 minutes, until the sultanas are plump and the nuts lightly coloured.

Transfer the rice to a warmed serving dish and gently fork in the sultanas and nuts. Arrange the egg around the edge and sprinkle the coriander on top.

Serves 6

Biryani

8 tablespoons ghee*
   or oil
10 cm (4 inch) piece
   cinnamon stick*
8 whole cardamom*
12 cloves
4 cloves garlic,
   crushed
3.5 cm (1½ inch)
   piece ginger*,
   chopped
1 teaspoon fennel
   seeds*
½ teaspoon chilli
   powder*
1 kg (2 lb) boned leg
   of lamb, cubed
2 × 150 g (5.2 oz)
   cartons natural
   yogurt
150 ml (¼ pint)
   water
2 teaspoons salt
500 g (1 lb) Basmati
   rice, washed and
   soaked for 30
   minutes
½ teaspoon saffron
   threads*, soaked in
   3 tablespoons
   boiling water
TO GARNISH:
2 tablespoons ghee*
   or oil
1 large onion, sliced
4 tablespoons flaked
   almonds
4 tablespoons
   sultanas

Heat 6 tablespoons of the ghee or oil in a large saucepan. Add the cinnamon, cardamom and cloves and fry for a few seconds, stirring. When the spices let out a strong aroma, stir in the garlic, ginger, fennel and chilli powder. Fry for 5 minutes, stirring constantly.

Add the lamb and fry well on all sides. Stir in the yogurt a tablespoon at a time, allowing each spoonful to be absorbed before adding the next. Add the water and half the salt, cover and simmer for 40 minutes or until the lamb is tender.

Meanwhile, fill another large pan two thirds full with water and bring to the boil. Drain the rice and add to the pan with the remaining salt. Boil for 3 minutes, then drain.

Put the remaining ghee or oil in a large casserole, cover the base with rice and sprinkle with the saffron water, then cover with a layer of lamb. Repeat the layers, finishing with rice. Pour in any liquid from the lamb, cover closely with a foil-lined lid and cook in a preheated moderately hot oven, 190°C (375°F), Gas Mark 5, for 25 to 30 minutes or until the rice is tender.

Meanwhile, prepare the garnish. Heat the ghee or oil in a small frying pan, add the onion and fry until golden. Remove from the pan and set aside. Add the almonds and sultanas to the pan and fry until the almonds are lightly coloured and the sultanas plump.

Transfer the biryani to a warmed serving dish and sprinkle with the onion, almonds and sultanas to serve.
Serves 4 to 6

Pilau Rice

3 tablespoons oil
5 cm (2 inch) piece
   cinnamon stick*
4 cardamom*
4 cloves
1 onion, sliced
250 g (8 oz) long-
   grain rice, washed
   and soaked for
   30 minutes
600 ml (1 pint) beef
   stock or water
salt

Heat the oil in a casserole, add the cinnamon, cardamom and cloves and fry for a few seconds. Add the onion and fry until golden. Drain the rice thoroughly, add to the pan and fry, stirring occasionally, for 5 minutes. Add the stock or water, and salt to taste. Bring to the boil, then simmer, uncovered, for 10 minutes, until the rice is tender and the liquid absorbed.

Serves 4

Illustrated on page 26

VARIATION:

Vegetable Pilau: Add 125 g (4 oz) each shelled peas, thinly sliced carrots and cauliflower florets to the pan after frying the onion. Fry for 5 minutes, then add the rice and proceed as above.

BREADS

Paratha

250 g (8 oz)
   wholemeal flour
1 teaspoon salt
200 ml (⅓ pint)
   water
   (approximately)
50-75 g (2-3 oz)
   melted ghee* or
   butter

Make the dough as for Chapati
(opposite) and divide into 6 pieces.
Roll out each piece on a floured
surface into a thin circle. Brush with
melted ghee or butter and fold in half;
brush again and fold in half again.
Roll out again to a circle about 3 mm
(⅛ inch) thick.

Lightly grease a griddle or heavy-
based frying pan with a little ghee or
butter and place over a moderate
heat. Add a paratha and cook for
1 minute. Lightly brush the top with
a little ghee or butter and turn over.
Brush all round the edge with ghee or
butter and cook until golden.
Remove from the pan and keep warm
while cooking the rest. Serve hot.
Makes 6

Chapati

250 g (8 oz)
 wholemeal flour
1 teaspoon salt
200 ml (⅓ pint)
 water
 (approximately)

Place the flour and salt in a bowl.
Make a well in the centre, gradually
stir in the water and work to a soft
supple dough. Knead for 10 minutes,
then cover and leave in a cool place
for 30 minutes. Knead again very
thoroughly, then divide into
12 pieces. Roll out each piece on a
floured surface into a thin round
pancake.

Lightly grease a griddle or heavy-
based frying pan with a little ghee* or
oil and place over a moderate heat.
Add a chapati and cook until blisters ·
appear. Press down with a fish slice,
then turn and cook the other side
until lightly coloured. Remove from
the pan and keep warm while
cooking the rest.

Brush a little butter on one side
and serve warm.
Makes 12

Puri

250 g (8 oz)
    wholemeal flour,
    or half wholemeal
    and half plain
    white
1/4 teaspoon salt
150 ml (1/4 pint)
    warm water
    (approximately)
2 teaspoons melted
    ghee*
oil for deep-frying

Place the wholemeal flour and salt in
a bowl; sift in the plain flour if using.
Make a well in the centre, add the
water gradually and work to a dough.
Knead in the ghee, then knead for
10 minutes, until smooth and elastic.
Cover and set aside for 30 minutes.

Divide the dough into 16 pieces.
With lightly oiled hands, pat each
piece into a ball. Lightly oil the pastry
board and rolling pin and roll out
each ball into a thin circular pancake.

Deep-fry the puris very quickly,
turning them over once, until deep
golden in colour. Drain well and
serve immediately.
Makes 16

Naan

15 g (½ oz) fresh
  yeast
¼ teaspoon sugar
2 tablespoons warm
  water
500 g (1 lb) self-
  raising flour
1 teaspoon salt
150 ml (¼ pint)
  tepid milk
150 ml (¼ pint)
  natural yogurt (at
  room temperature)
2 tablespoons melted
  butter or cooking
  oil
TO GARNISH:
2-3 tablespoons
  melted butter
1 tablespoon poppy
  or sesame seeds

Put the yeast in a small bowl with the sugar and water. Mix well until the yeast has dissolved, then leave in a warm place for 15 minutes or until the mixture is frothy.

Sift the flour and salt into a large bowl. Make a well in the centre and pour in the yeast, milk, yogurt and butter or oil. Mix well to a smooth dough and turn onto a floured surface. Knead well for about 10 minutes, until smooth and elastic. Place in the bowl, cover with clingfilm and leave to rise in a warm place for 1 to 1½ hours, or until doubled in size.

Turn onto a floured surface, knead for a few minutes, then divide into 6 pieces. Pat or roll each piece into a round.

Place on a warmed baking sheet and bake in a preheated very hot oven, 240°C (475°F), Gas Mark 9, for 10 minutes. Brush with butter and sprinkle with the poppy or sesame seeds. Serve warm.
Makes 6

ACCOMPANIMENTS

Carrot Salad

125 g (4 oz) carrots,
  grated
25 g (1 oz) grated
  onion
1/2 tablespoon grated
  ginger*
1 tablespoon finely
  chopped mint
1/2 teaspoon salt
1/2 teaspoon sugar
1 tablespoon lemon
  juice

Mix all the ingredients together,
cover and chill for 1 to 2 hours before
serving.
Serves 4

Raita

100 g (3½ oz)
  cucumber, thinly
  sliced
salt
2 × 150 g (5.2 oz)
  cartons natural
  yogurt
50 g (2 oz) spring
  onions, thinly
  sliced
1 green chilli*, seeded
  and finely chopped
coriander leaves*, to
  garnish

Place the cucumber in a colander,
sprinkle with salt and leave to drain
for 30 minutes. Dry thoroughly.

Mix the yogurt with salt to taste
and fold in the cucumber, spring
onion and chilli. Arrange in a serving
dish and chill until required. Garnish
with coriander leaves to serve.

Serves 4

NOTE: Raita can be made with other
vegetables and with fruit – bananas
are particularly good.

Cachumber

1 onion, chopped
250 g (8 oz)
   tomatoes, skinned
   and chopped
1-2 green chillies*,
   chopped
1-2 tablespoons
   vinegar
salt

Put the onion, tomatoes and chillies
in a dish. Pour over the vinegar (the
mixture must not be too liquid) and
add salt to taste. Chill before serving.
Serves 4

Mango Chutney

1 kg (2 lb) very firm
   mangoes
500 g (1 lb) sugar
600 ml (1 pint)
   vinegar
5 cm (2 inch) piece
   ginger*
4 cloves garlic
½-1 tablespoon chilli
   powder*
1 tablespoon mustard
   seeds*
2 tablespoons salt
125 g (4 oz) raisins
   or sultanas

Peel the mangoes and cut into small
pieces; set aside.

Place the sugar and all but 1
tablespoon of the vinegar in a pan and
simmer for 10 minutes.

Place the ginger, garlic and
remaining vinegar in an electric
blender or food processor and work
to a paste. Add to the pan and cook
for 10 minutes, stirring.

Add the mango and remaining
ingredients and cook, uncovered, for
about 25 minutes, stirring as the
chutney thickens.

Pour into hot sterilized jars, cover
with waxed discs, then seal with
cellophane covers and label. The
chutney will keep for several months.
Makes about 1.25 kg (2½ lb)

Zalata

250 g (8 oz) ridge
  cucumbers, peeled
  and sliced
salt
1 green chilli*, sliced
1 tablespoon finely
  chopped coriander*
2 tablespoons vinegar
½ teaspoon sugar

Place the cucumber in a colander,
sprinkle with salt and leave to drain
for 30 minutes. Dry thoroughly.
Place in a serving dish and add the
remaining ingredients and 1 teaspoon
salt. Mix well and chill thoroughly
before serving.

Alternatively, place the drained
cucumber in an electric blender or
food processor with the whole chilli,
coriander leaves, sugar and salt. Add
1 clove garlic and just ½ tablespoon
vinegar and work to a smooth paste.
Chill thoroughly before serving.
Serves 4

Coriander Chutney

25 g (1 oz) desiccated
   coconut
1 × 150 g (5.2 oz)
   carton natural
   yogurt
100 g (3½ oz)
   coriander*, including
   some fine stalks
2 green chillies*
juice of 1 lemon
1 teaspoon salt
1 teaspoon sugar

Mix the coconut with the yogurt and leave to stand for 1 hour. Place in an electric blender or food processor with the remaining ingredients and work until smooth. Chill before serving.
Serves 4

Prawn Relish

2 tablespoons oil
1 onion, chopped
4 dried red chillies*
2 green chillies*,
   chopped
½ teaspoon cumin
   seeds*
½ teaspoon turmeric*
1 clove garlic, crushed
2.5 cm (1 inch) piece
   ginger*, chopped
4 curry leaves*,
   crumbled
150 g (5 oz) prawns
1 tablespoon vinegar
salt

Heat the oil in a pan, add the onion and fry until golden. Crumble in the dried chillies. Add the fresh chillies, cumin, turmeric, garlic, ginger and curry leaves and fry for 2 minutes. Add the prawns and fry for 2 minutes.

Add the vinegar and salt to taste and simmer, uncovered, for 3 to 4 minutes, until most of the liquid has evaporated. Serve hot or cold.
Serves 4

Date and Tomato Chutney

250 g (8 oz) dates,
   stoned and chopped
1 × 539 g (1 lb 3 oz)
   can tomatoes
1 onion, chopped
3.5 cm (1½ inch)
   piece ginger*,
   chopped
1 teaspoon chilli
   powder*
1 teaspoon salt
6 tablespoons vinegar

Put all the ingredients in a saucepan and stir well. Bring to the boil, then simmer, uncovered, for about 45 minutes, stirring occasionally, until thick. Serve cold.
Serves 4 to 6
NOTE: Extra chilli powder and salt may be added if wished, according to taste.

DESSERTS & SWEET MEATS

Semolina Barfi

50 g (2 oz) fine
  semolina
125 g (4 oz) sugar
450 ml (¾ pint)
  milk
50 g (2 oz) butter
10 cardamom*,
  peeled and crushed
75 g (3 oz) blanched
  almonds, halved
  and toasted

Place the semolina and sugar in a
heavy-based pan and stir in the milk
gradually until smooth. Add the
butter in small pieces. Bring to the
boil, stirring, then simmer for 3 to
4 minutes, until thickened, stirring
occasionally to prevent sticking. Add
the cardamom and continue cooking
for another 10 minutes until the
mixture leaves the side of the pan.

Spread on a buttered plate or dish
to a thickness of 1 to 1.5 cm (½ to
1 inch). Leave until almost cold, then
decorate with the almonds.

Serve cold, cut into slices or
squares.

Serves 4 to 6

Kheer

75 g (3 oz) long-
    grain rice
1.75 litres (3 pints)
    milk
50 g (2 oz) sultanas
    (optional)
caster sugar to taste
142 ml (5 fl oz)
    single cream
flaked almonds or
    lightly crushed
    cardamom seeds*
    to decorate

Place the rice and 1 litre (1¾ pints) of the milk in a heavy-based pan. Cook gently at simmering point for 45 minutes to 1 hour, until most of the milk has been absorbed.

Add the remaining milk and the sultanas, if using, stir well and continue simmering until thickened. Remove from the heat and add sugar to taste.

Leave until completely cold, stirring occasionally to prevent a skin forming, then stir in the cream.

Turn into small dishes and serve cold, sprinkled with flaked almonds or crushed cardamom seeds.

Serves 4

Almond Barfi

750 ml (1¼ pints)
 milk
50 g (2 oz) caster
 sugar
50 g (2 oz) ground
 almonds
6 cardamom*, peeled
 and crushed

Reduce the milk as for Mawa (see page 93).

When it is thick and lumpy, stir in the sugar, then add the almonds and cook for 2 minutes. Spread on a buttered plate and sprinkle with the crushed cardamom. Serve warm, cut into wedges or diamond shapes.
Serves 4

Shrikand

1 kg (2.2 lb) natural
 yogurt
1 packet powdered
 saffron
about 2 tablespoons
 caster sugar
about 1 tablespoon
 rose water
TO DECORATE:
1-2 teaspoons
 cardamom seeds*,
 crushed
1 tablespoon pistachio
 nuts, shelled and
 chopped

Turn the yogurt into a strainer lined with muslin and leave to drip over a bowl for 6 hours. Put the dried curds – there will be about 300 g (10 oz) – into a bowl and beat in the saffron. Add the sugar and taste; add a little more if you like, but it should not be too sweet. Mix in the rose water, a little at a time, until the mixture resembles thick cream. Cover and chill until required.

Spoon into individual bowls and decorate with the cardamom and pistachio nuts to serve.
Serves 4

Mawa

1.75 litres (3 pints)
  full cream milk
3-4 tablespoons caster
  sugar

Cook the milk in large, heavy-based saucepan for about 1¼ hours, until it is reduced to a thick lumpy consistency. Stir occasionally and be careful not to let the milk burn.

Add the sugar and continue cooking for 10 minutes.

Spread the mixture on a lightly buttered plate: it should be a light cream coloured, softly-set toffee.

Cut into wedges and serve cold.

Serves 4 to 6

Carrot Halva

1.2 litres (2 pints)
  milk
250 g (8 oz) carrot,
  finely grated
75 g (3 oz) butter
1 tablespoon golden
  syrup
125 g (4 oz) sugar
50 g (2 oz) sultanas
  or raisins
1 teaspoon cardamom
  seeds*, crushed, to
  decorate

Place the milk and carrots in a heavy-based saucepan and cook over high heat, stirring occasionally, until the liquid has evaporated. Add the butter, syrup, sugar and fruit. Stir until the butter and sugar have melted, then cook for 15 to 20 minutes, stirring frequently, until the mixture starts to leave the side of the pan.

Pour into a shallow buttered dish and spread evenly. Sprinkle with crushed cardamom. Cut into slices and serve warm or cold.

Serves 4 to 6

INDEX